The Matter of Families
New and Selected Poems

Robert H. Deluty

For Cindy
With love
+
warmest wishes
for your health
and happiness,
John

D1595934

Ben Yehuda Press
Teaneck, New Jersey

Published by Ben Yehuda Press
122 Ayers Court #1B
Teaneck, NJ 07666

http://www.BenYehudaPress.com

To subscribe to our monthly book club and support independent Jewish publishing, visit https://www.patreon.com/BenYehudaPress

Jewish Poetry Project #28   **http://jpoetry.us**

Ben Yehuda Press books may be purchased at a discount by synagogues, book clubs, and other institutions buying in bulk. For information, please email markets@BenYehudaPress.com

Library of Congress Cataloging-in-Publication Data

Names: Deluty, Robert H., author.
Title: The matter of families : new and selected poems / Robert H. Deluty.
Description: Teaneck, NJ : Ben Yehuda Press, [2022] | Series: Jewish poetry
  project ; #28 | Summary: "An exploration the many layers that bind us to
  tradition, faith, customs and, more than anything else, to the people
  that represent this visceral and often inexplicable connection: our
  loved-ones, our relatives, our next-of-kin"-- Provided by publisher.
Identifiers: LCCN 2022024690 | ISBN 9781953829337 (paperback)
Subjects: LCGFT: Poetry.
Classification: LCC PS3554.E4456 M38 2022 | DDC 811/.54--dc23/
eng/20220524
LC record available at https://lccn.loc.gov/2022024690

ISBN13 978-1-953829-33-7

22 23 24 / 10 9 8 7 6 5 4 3 2 1   202220524

In loving memory of

Barbara Medine Deluty,
David Deluty and
Elise (Kreppel) Deluty

Contents

Lessons

He loved to tell the story of how,
On his first day of Yeshiva
In Poland's Jewish Ghetto,
Mothers brought honey cakes,
Shaped like the letters of the
Hebrew alphabet,
So that their children
Would come to associate
Learning with sweetness.

A brilliant man, deprived by war
Of even a high school education,
He set foot on a college campus
More than fifty years later to attend
His first son's PhD conferral.
When introduced to the faculty,
With utmost respect and pleasure,
He bowed.

His second son, now a professor,
Remembers these stories
As he teaches his daughter
Her ABCs.

Wedding Dance

The bride and groom sit in the
Center of concentric circles.
Surrounding them, hand-in-hand,
Dance the major players in their lives:
Childhood pals, former classmates.
First cousins, new friends.
Uncles, aunts, teachers, colleagues.
Siblings, mother, father.
Threads from different eras and places
Woven together for a few minutes,
Forming a set of familial, communal
Identity bracelets.

Robert H. Deluty

What's in a Name?

Upon learning
from their elated son
their newborn grandchild
has been named Luca,
Mrs. Leibowitz bemoans
that her only association
is to the abused child in the
Suzanne Vega song, whereas
Mr. Leibowitz laments
that his only association
is to the Corleone enforcer
who sleeps with the fish

Entitlement

Entitled
>To rage because of insult
>To hate because of mistreatment
>To steal because of deprivation
>To destroy and be destroyed

Or

Ennobled
>With a single, precious entitlement,
>One's birthright as a human being:
>To be respected

Robert H. Deluty

Bertha

Romanian-born, 58 inches tall,
Fractured English, cherished family.
Obsessively neat, worried relentlessly,
Ended each good-bye with *Be careful*.
When her grandson went off to Buffalo,
Fretted about him alone in *Siberia*.
Lived selflessly, died beloved.

Six-Year-Old Theologian

Uncommonly solemn
He sadly concludes
There's one thing
God simply can't do –
Have a birthday party

Robert H. Deluty

Senryu

a Jew eating ham
hoping his deceased father
is not watching

ancient Greek scholars
swapping their favorite
Yiddish proverbs

Vassar Marxists
naming their firstborn child
Fidel Feinberg

Brandeis Marxists
naming their firstborn child
Ho Chi Minsky

a Jewish convert
in labor, delivering
her first *oy*

Senryu

Jewish punk rocker,
half his head shaved, tries to keep
his yarmulke on

Hebrew School class
appeals to the Mets' owner
for kosher franks

on Yom Kippur
four friends rate their mothers
on guilt-induction

Auschwitz survivor
sharing his wartime stories
with Vietnam vets

a country club
proudly accepting its first
Jewish caddie

Senryu

elderly rabbi
dreams of being the victor
in a bar fight

a twelve-year-old Jew
wonders if Jesus had fun
at *his* Bar Mitzvah

the Goldman brothers
dubbing their banjo efforts
Jewgrass music

ninety-sixth birthday . . .
Great-Uncle Sy belting out
Wild Thing

Aunt Brooke confiding
their last name Wellingham
was once Welkowitz

For Elise and David

By deeds and by words
They would show and tell:
Be caring, be competent.
Do good and do well.

Nietzsche & Mrs. Berg

What doesn't kill us
Makes us stronger.
In her hospital bed
The septuagenarian,
Ravaged by
Arthritis,
Diabetes,
Depression and
Sarcoma, reads
These famous words
And begs to differ.

A Mother's Gift

Pregnancy with you was a pleasure.
And, during your delivery,
I actually laughed out loud –
Your feather-soft head of hair
Tickled me so as the doctor
Pulled you from me.

Such was my mother's rendition
Of the story of my birth.
Partly fact, mostly fantasy,
Largely reflecting a selfless wish
That her middle child feel welcome,
Special, loved.

Name Calling

Recent birth announcements
Evoke a frightening epiphany:
In 60 years, most grandmas
Will be named Ashley and Tiffany.

Empathy

One-year-old,
Teething, miserable,
Refuses to suffer quietly.
Mother tries every trick:
Each is met with tears, tantrums.
Exhausted, hopeless,
Mother screams, then sobs.
Seeing an adult cry
For the first time,
Child quiets down,
Hands mother her bottle.

Senryu

goes to the market
just to hear another voice:
Paper or plastic?

tears fall silently
as she fills the new lunch box
of her last-born child

public library . . .
a child searches under C
for coloring books

going blind,
she tries to memorize
her grandsons' faces

learning is rebirth:
start of school, Jewish new year
coincide each fall

Senryu

Alzheimer parents
now, nursing home roommates –
together, alone

plastic slipcovers
adorning broken chairs . . .
Nana's living room

his wife
reading a romance novel
at the ballgame

three televisions
in a family's home . . .
the same program

at the checkout . . .
old man sees a young beauty,
hides the bran flakes

Robert H. Deluty

Disconnected

The near-deaf elder
Struggling mightily to hear.
The newly verbal toddler
Groping to make desires known.
Both rageful . . .
One unable to understand,
The other, to be understood.

Second Born

Fewer arrival gifts,
Shorter journal entries,
Quarter as many photographs.
Yet,
No less loved,
No less treasured,
No less a miracle.

Robert H. Deluty

Thankless

He prays for a promotion
To the executive suite;
He gets a drunken driver
Missing him by inches.
She prays for the strength
To lose five pounds;
She gets a heartfelt letter
From a long-lost friend.
They pray for the world
To take note of their talent;
They get a day with their children
Filled with laughter and trust.

They pray for the trivial,
They get the wondrous,
Yet they ask
Why weren't our prayers answered?

Juggler

Mother, spouse, wage earner –
Roles, like juggled balls,
Forming fluid intersecting arcs.
Distance, balance, emphasis
Are relentlessly adjusted so that
None is over- or under-stressed.
Roles that must be humble,
Each willing and able
To relinquish apogee
To maintain equilibrium.

Robert H. Deluty

Encores

The greatest hits of
Long-forgotten recordings –
I'll give you something to cry about!
Why are you doing this to me?
This is your very last warning! –
Are reflexively retrieved
As their children repeat
Their own classic routines.

Champion

Each day provides
Seventeen sleepless hours.
Each hour, a boxing round.
Depression, the opponent.
Jabs hopelessness, dejection.
Absorbs counterpunches of doubt,
Uppercuts suicidal ideation.
Withstands daily punishment,
Both self- and other-inflicted.
Yet refuses to retire from the ring.

Robert H. Deluty

Valentines

Her face is perfectly round,
Her mother's, elegantly angular.
Yet both radiate sweetness,
Exuberance and delight.

Her eyes are dark brown almonds,
Her mother's, deep blue globes.
Yet both find joys and pleasures
That others fail to see.

Her arms are short and chubby,
Her mother's, long and willowy.
Yet both offer hugs and caresses
Of incomparable tenderness.

A Korean-born daughter,
A Long Island-reared mother,
Alike in all the important ways.

Senryu

Sidney Mermelstein
requesting that his nephews
call him *El Sid*

asking Uncle Irv
why Jews are surnamed Gold,
Silver, but not Bronze

asking Aunt Sheila
why Jews are surnamed Pearl,
Ruby, but not Jade

asking Grandpa Mel
why Jews are surnamed Stein,
Stern, but not Stallone

Sam Cohn believing
all wisecracks are funnier
with Yiddish accents

Robert H. Deluty

Senryu

the rabbi's wife
combing scores of matzo flakes
from his chest-length beard

Mrs. Washington
informing the young bigot
she was born Rose Katz

in Sunday School
two fifth graders debating
the souls of gerbils

mid-nightmare . . .
an Orthodox rabbi
shucking oysters

new Nazi defeat . . .
death camp survivor teaching
his grandchild Hebrew

Senryu

Jewish five-year-old
calling his teenaged tutor
Rabbi

Mrs. Weiss noting
why she drinks no alcohol:
Blocks my suffering

new Holy Cross prof,
a Jew, wishing the teams
were not Crusaders

his Sikh R.A.
reminding Dr. Feldstein
today's Yom Kippur

Aunt Lil swearing
she spotted Pope Francis
at Bernstein's Deli

Senryu

on Rosh Hashanah
the Jewish pro-bowler
getting his ninth split

Murray Weiss giving
fifty dollars to *Goodwill*
after eating shrimp

far-left professor
excoriating Israel,
ignoring ISIS

second grade classroom . . .
amidst holly and reindeer,
one small dreidel

death camp survivor
reviews Holocaust movie:
Actors were too fat

For Elise

In her twenties,
One of the best diamond cutters
In New York City.
A decade later,
Effortlessly able to spot a dime
On a child's bedroom floor
Littered with toys and clothes.
Now, legally blind,
Unable to open a dictionary
And find the meaning of *irony*.

Corner Store, 1966

Jet-black-wigged Anna, 70,
Stood all day behind the counter,
Reading newspapers cover-to-cover,
Reluctantly looking up to make change,
Milkshakes or small talk.

Zig, her husband of a half-century
And dispositional opposite, greeted
Each patron with a smiling,
Heavily accented, *Nu, h'war you, pal?*
Before launching into an impromptu,
Disjointed oration on world events.

With a dime in hand, I'd visit
Anna-and-Zig's each school day –
To indulge in their licorice whips,
Halvah, and chocolate-covered jellies,
To escape all responsibility,
To taste sweetness and to smile.

Senryu

drama class . . .
Chinese students rehearsing
Fiddler on the Roof

Bronx Jew in Duluth
struggling to comprehend
lemon *Jell-o*

post Bar Mitzvah...
asking permission to cut
his own bread crusts

odd-numbered candles,
even numbered children . . .
Hanukkah fractions

mid-Passover . . .
Jewish woman going through
doughnut withdrawal

Robert H. Deluty

Senryu

faculty lounge . . .
two Southern Methodist profs
chatting in Yiddish

Auschwitz survivor
stares at his grandson's arm:
skull-and-bones tattoo

thin rainbow candles
aglow in December's cold . . .
Hanukkah sundown

centenarian,
3-month-old great-granddaughter
exchange toothless smiles

Christmas tradition . . .
Jewish family dining
with chopsticks

Senryu

Jewish matron
teaching her punk granddaughter
the rules of mah-jongg

Passover's third night . . .
a Queens bagel store owner
flying to Cancun

Baylor-DePaul game . . .
relaxed Jews sitting amongst
Baptists, Catholics

nine-year-old Dan Klein
wonders if smelling bacon
is a sin

two Jewish mothers
discussing the benefits
of shame and guilt

Robert H. Deluty

Father and Son

He died. He was too young
To experience retirement
And daughters-in-law;
To enjoy grandchildren
And peace of mind.

He died. I was too young
To ask him to describe in detail
His parents and childhood,
Dreams and disappointments;
To tell him directly that
My pride in him was surpassed
Only by my love for him.

Both too young. Now too late.

Survivor's Handball

Said he loved the game
Because the ball was like
His heart – dark, hard, small.
He would hit each shot
At full strength, as if trying to make
The ball's blackness explode.
As if each strike
Might crack open
A dark, hard, small heart
Forged by pain, loss.

Robert H. Deluty

Passover Seder

Each Spring, loved ones gather
To extol and thank God for
Miracles past and present;
To partake matzo and wine,
Salt water and bitter herbs;
To recount Israelite servitude,
Exodus and redemption; and
To rejoice in the world's
Most precious gifts:
Freedom and children.

David and David

Bringed,
For him and I,
The men what went,
Catastrophe pronounced *cat-is-truff* . . .
The six year-old's errors of spelling,
Grammar, pronunciation, and usage
Echo those made by
The Polish-born grandfather
He never had a chance to meet.

Eraser

Had them removed
As soon as he arrived.
Before learning the language,
Buying a suit, or
Making a friend.
Viewed it as vital
To bleach the past,
To pass as American.
Instead of blue numbers, now
He had scars on a forearm
To match the scars within.

Balance

Old story:
— The secret to your long and happy marriage?
My wife makes all minor decisions, and
I'm responsible for all major ones.
— Minor decisions?
Like, should we buy or rent?
How should we discipline the children?
Where should we invest our savings?
Should we put Mom in a nursing home?
— And your *major* decisions?
Is there a God?
How do we achieve racial harmony?
What is the meaning of life?

Current story:
A marriage of equal partners, with each
Balancing career *and* family.
Providing child care *and* public service.
Delighting in the mysteries of God *and* of
2-year-olds.
Working to lessen strife among nations *and*
Between siblings.
Seeking solace in the Great Books *and* a
Spouse's caress.
Taking time to search for philosophic truths *and*
For a little girl's missing sneakers.
Striving to have it all, but
Without any delusion of achieving it.

Robert H. Deluty

Bedtime Questions

Why don't I have grandparents?
—*They died years ago.*
How'd they die?
—*They were killed by the Nazis.*
Why?
—*Because they were Jews.*
What difference did that make?
—*At the time, it made all the difference
 in the world.*
At school, a girl said that God never gives us
 more than we can handle. Didn't God give
 your parents too much?
—*Go to sleep. Sweet dreams.*

Glory Days in the Bronx

It was our reward for perfect
Attendance in Hebrew School:
A day trip to Yankee Stadium.
Proudly, gleefully, we'd leave
Our public schools at noon, and
Rendezvous at the synagogue.
From there, a 3-block walk and
A 5-stop subway ride to
River Avenue and 161st Street.

Upon entering the stadium
We put on our Yankee caps,
Akin to donning our
Yarmulkes in temple.
Each of us held a
Baseball glove in one hand, a
Paper-bagged lunch in the other
(Ballpark franks, though enticing,
Alas, were not Kosher.) To us, it
Couldn't have mattered less whom
The Yanks were playing that day;
We could barely see the players
From our faraway bleacher seats.
What *did* matter was that
We were with our friends,
Laughing, joking, screaming,
Breathing beer-scented air
On a school day in May.
Welcome guests in the home of
Whitey and Yogi, Mickey and Roger.

Robert H. Deluty

Senryu

three Polish Jews
walking through Arlington,
offering thanks

on Yom Kippur
their unorthodox uncle
eating foods he hates

death camp survivor
teaching her great-granddaughters
the joy of blintzes

a celiac patient
willing to pay the price
for a marble rye

a Jew in Quebec
befriending a Christian girl
named Goyette

Senryu

Saul Cahn explaining
why his middle name is Xing:
Nana is Chinese

Jewish man screaming
at his spouse for muttering
You're my cross to bear

Sol Blume asking God
why He made sardines kosher,
but not lobster

Grandma Ida
describing her young neighbor
as a *sexypot*

ten-year-old Jake Stein
inquiring whether a wench
is a woman mensch

Robert H. Deluty

Senryu

Aunt Sylvia
referring to herself as
a seltzer snob

Uncles Milt and Max
presenting themselves as
matzo ball mavens

bagel shop owner
informing a young patron
it's *schmear*, not *smear*

in Paris, Aunt Rose
pronouncing a typed *Oui*
as *Oy*

young Zev Cohn asking
why Jews eat horseradish
willingly

With Age

Observing her father

At 32, building their home with his own hands,
Wondering if he'll live forever.

At 46, asking for help after breaking his leg,
Perceiving him as mortal.

At 59, terrified after his first heart attack,
Regarding him as fragile.

At 74, profoundly depressed after his stroke,
Fearing he's at death's door.

At 93, caressing his newest great-grandchild,
Wondering if he'll live forever.

Robert H. Deluty

Senryu

Jewish boys debate
how long to sit Shiva
for a dead hamster

Passover seder . . .
ADHD child posing
only two questions

the DJ playing
at their nephew's Bar Mitzvah
Springsteen's *I'm on Fire*

Aunt Ruth asking God
to deliver a few plagues
to Capitol Hill

a Jewish man
asserting he's Orthodox
one day a year

Senryu

Queens kosher deli . . .
the Maine tourist requesting
a wine list

Queens kosher deli . . .
the Kansas tourist asking
for buttered white toast

St. Patrick's Day . . .
Dad introducing himself
as Ben O'Levy

discovering
the R&B hit was penned
by Sarah Goldfarb

two Jews in Vail
debating which couple
looks most Goyish

Robert H. Deluty

Vaudevillian

I heard on the radio that
an old-time comic had died.
As a boy, I used to watch him
on *The Ed Sullivan Show* with
my parents on Sunday nights.
I hated his loud clothes,
foreign accents, mincing walk,
interminable set-ups, and
obvious punchlines.
Yet, I felt a deep sadness
at his passing . . .
He made my father laugh.

Senryu

a Gentile lady
in a Jewish bakery
requesting *holly*

for no good reason,
young Josh Katz begins speaking
with a Thai accent

Aunt Syl noting
Uncle Mort often makes
misspokements

Jewish heretic
reading *Portnoy's Complaint*
on Rosh Hashanah

old Jew refusing
to eat porcini mushrooms:
Too close to pork

Senryu

with mixed feelings
watching a young Israeli
conducting Wagner

nine-year-old Meyer,
living in Brooklyn, asking
to be called Tex

in shul . . . Finkelstein
telling Weiss he'll clobber him
once Yom Kippur ends

Rachel Blume teaching
her Lutheran neighbors how
kvetch and *kvell* differ

Max Cohen teaching
his Methodist neighbors how
schmuck and *schnook* differ

Senryu

Jewish bride
walking down the aisle
as bagpipes play

the caterer
regarding Bar Mitzvahs as
parties of thirteen

for Hanukkah,
Kaplan's Baptist wife making
gingerbread latkes

Aunt Golda giving
each trick-or-treater
five raisins

a Jewish child
assuming the *n-word*
is *nudnik*

Senryu

a child questioning
if kosher beef comes from cows
raised by rabbis

Chinese New Year . . .
Dr. Stein wishing Nurse Zhang
a *Shanah Tovah*

his wife mistaking
Leopold and Loeb for
Lerner and Loewe

Halloween night . . .
nine Yeshiva boys dressed
as a menorah

old Jewish waiter
wishing sarcasm alone
could pay his bills

Senryu

in shul, Uncle Sol
sporting mauve shorts, white *Keds*,
a black fedora

Mimi Goldman
calling her baby daughter
Mini Mi

a child questioning
the rabbi must her turtle
keep kosher

young Jewish Texan
blanching upon learning what
Corpus Christi means

Isaac Kahn
wanting to name his son
Genghis

Robert H. Deluty

Senryu

three rabbis
on St. Patrick's Day
sharing slivovitz

the cantor
trying to convince his son
shrimp tastes like tuna

in court, Sid Shulman
defending the skinhead
who wishes him dead

Jewish French chef
preparing a crepe du jour
filled with kasha

maternity ward . . .
Dachau survivor welcomes
his sixth great-grandchild

Perfectionist

Anxious when working,
Guilty if shirking.
Fearing heightened expectations
When work is commendable,
Dreading disapproving gazes
For efforts lamentable.
And should perfection be achieved,
Comfort is painfully brief,
For a fall from grace is awaited,
Stifling hope of lasting relief

50 Years after Auschwitz

At night,
Alone in his chair,
What did he see when
Staring out the window?
His mother's face –
Warm, serene
Or pale, gaunt?
Friday night dinner –
Boiled beef and horseradish
Or thin, rancid broth?
Smoke –
Coming from his father's pipe
Or from the crematoria?
To protect us, he never shared.
To spare him, we never asked.

Getting It

To be content, I must create.
A work of art, of literature, of science;
Something unique, something my own.
And to be happy, truly happy,
My creation must be recognized,
Acclaimed and enduring.

How sad, his wife replied,
That evoking a smile, teaching a lesson,
Watching a sunset, relieving a burden
Provide you with neither contentment
Nor happiness.

You don't get it, he shouted.
Thank goodness, she sighed.

Robert H. Deluty

Senryu

Easter morning . . .
the cantor telling his spouse
Good yontif

career criminals
naming their newborn twins
Cain and Ahab

Day of Atonement . . .
young David Katz requesting
just one *Reese's Piece*

the rabbi noting
Boaz, before he married,
was *Ruthless*

a Catholic girl
wishing her Jewish friend
a fun Yom Kippur

Senryu

Yeshiva student
asking if the Phoenicians
invented blinds

Yeshiva student
asking who was better:
Moses or Jesus

Yeshiva student
asking if God watches us
in the shower

Yeshiva student
asking what dinosaurs ate
on Noah's ark

Yeshiva student
asking if the math's hard in
the Book of Numbers

Robert H. Deluty

Senryu

Yom Kippur morning . . .
Melvin Klein viewing himself
as *Mel atonin'*

Gentile houseguest
hunting through Levy's fridge
for some bacon

What rhymes with toy? . . .
Grandpa Mort answering *Goy;*
Grandma Frieda, *Oy*

Aunt Miriam
calling her son's daughters
the grandangels

Aunt Miriam
calling her daughter's sons
the four stooges

Senryu

Day of Atonement . . .
the half-Jewish Turk
drinking decaf

tennis champion
requesting a bagel
that's top-seeded

Rabbi Blume calling
his teenaged sons, now driving,
schlemiels on wheels

Great-Grandma Sophie
referring to sweet gherkins
as *Gentile pickles*

Hebrew School teacher,
asked *What's an ark?*, replying
A couples' cruise ship

Senryu

asking the rabbi
what their poodle should eat
during Passover

debutantes walk in
on the Stein Bar Mitzvah ...
wrong banquet hall

Judo master Lee,
a Jewish convert, hearing
a Holocaust joke

Sunday School ...
a nine year-old demanding
hard evidence

at a wishing well
pondering the downside
of eternal life

Senryu

the Jewish chef
portraying Passover as
a feast without yeast

on her deathbed
pondering which child will give
the worst eulogy

Uncle Max noting
a money belt is where
cash goes to waist

the pre-K child
informing Grandpa Izzy
what *hangry* means

Grandpa Izzy
informing the pre-K child
what *kvetch* means

History Lesson

First, the elder explains
To his grandchildren
What a typewriter is.

Next, he describes
Sitting in a classroom
With twenty-nine other
Seventh graders learning
To peck at the keyboard of
A manual *Smith Corona.*

Finally, he relates how,
Because of his visual-motor
Ineptitude, he nearly failed
The class, eking out a low *D*
By turning in on the final day
Of the grading period
An extra-credit report on
The history of the typewriter
Which he wrote in longhand.

Toddlersaurus

Lurching, lumbering, careening flat-footed,
Oblivious to obstacles and dangers in its path.
Hurtling head-on single-mindedly,
Arms flailing, fingers jabbing,
Mouth, tongue, and teeth primed and ready.
Wide-eyed, wild-eyed,
An admixture of delight, wonder, and purpose.
An early life form
Taking its first unassisted steps.

Connections

Ya know what an organism is?
It's an individual living system.
Ya know why I love New York City?
Because it's organic!
Just look at this subway map —
It's like a circulatory system.
Blood flows through the train lines.
A, B, D, F, 1, 2, 4, 6, 7, J, L, Q, Z.
The North Bronx is connected
To Coney Island, West Manhattan
To Forest Hills, Bedford-Stuyvesant
To Wall Street, Harlem to Astoria.
Head to toe, across the chest,
Up one arm, down the other.
Isn't that cool?!

We loved listening to Uncle Murray,
Beholding his madness and brilliance
Connect.

77290

I remember his left arm.
Leather-tough, lightly freckled,
Thick as a fireplace log.
Culminating in short, dense fingers
With near-perfectly round nails.
Most memorable, though, was the forearm,
Damaged by five blue numbers:
His concentration camp tattoo.
A daily/nightly reminder of
Evil and martyrdom,
Faith and resilience.

Robert H. Deluty

About the author

Dr. Robert H. Deluty is Associate Dean Emeritus of the Graduate School at the University of Maryland, Baltimore County. A psychology professor at UMBC from 1980 to 2016, he was named Presidential Teaching Professor in 2002. Dr. Deluty's poems and essays have been published in *The Wall Street Journal, The Baltimore Sun, The Pegasus Review, Modern Haiku, Voices: The Art and Science of Psychotherapy, Psychiatric Times, Jewish Currents, The Journal of Poetry Therapy, Welcome Home, Muse of Fire, Maryland Family Magazine, Gastronomica: The Journal of Food and Culture, The Faculty Voice*, and many other newspapers, journals, and anthologies. His 63rd book, *Sensations and Associations*, was published in February 2022.

The Jewish Poetry Project

jpoetry.us

Ben Yehuda Press

From the Coffee House of Jewish Dreamers: Poems of Wonder and Wandering and the Weekly Torah Portion by Isidore Century

"Isidore Century is a wonderful poet. His poems are funny, deeply observed, without pretension." – *The Jewish Week*

The House at the Center of the World: Poetic Midrash on Sacred Space by Abe Mezrich

"Direct and accessible, Mezrich's midrashic poems often tease profound meaning out of his chosen Torah texts. These poems remind us that our Creator is forgiving, that the spiritual and physical can inform one another, and that the supernatural can be carried into the everyday."
—Yehoshua November, author of *God's Optimism*

we who desire: Poems and Torah riffs by Sue Swartz

"Sue Swartz does magnificent acrobatics with the Torah. She takes the English that's become staid and boring, and adds something that's new and strange and exciting. These are poems that leave a taste in your mouth, and you walk away from them thinking, what did I just read? Oh, yeah. It's the Bible."
—Matthue Roth, author, *Yom Kippur A Go-Go*

Open My Lips: Prayers and Poems
by Rachel Barenblat

"Barenblat's God is a personal God—one who lets her cry on His shoulder, and who rocks her like a colicky baby. These poems bridge the gap between the ineffable and the human. This collection will bring comfort to those with a religion of their own, as well as those seeking a relationship with some kind of higher power."
—Satya Robyn, author, *The Most Beautiful Thing*

Words for Blessing the World: Poems in Hebrew and English by Herbert J. Levine

"These writings express a profoundly earth-based theology in a language that is clear and comprehensible. These are works to study and learn from."
—Rodger Kamenetz, author, *The Jew in the Lotus*

Shiva Moon: Poems by Maxine Silverman

"The poems, deeply felt, are spare, spoken in a quiet but compelling voice, as if we were listening in to her inner life. This book is a precious record of the transformation saying Kaddish can bring."
—Howard Schwartz, author, *The Library of Dreams*

is: heretical Jewish blessings and poems by Yaakov Moshe (Jay Michaelson)

"Finally, Torah that speaks to and through the lives we are actually living: expanding the tent of holiness to embrace what has been cast out, elevating what has been kept down, advancing what has been held back, reveling in questions, revealing contradictions."
—Eden Pearlstein, aka eprhyme

Texts to the Holy: Poems
by Rachel Barenblat

"These poems are remarkable, radiating a love of God that is full bodied, innocent, raw, pulsating, hot, drunk. I can hardly fathom their faith but am grateful for the vistas they open. I will sit with them, and invite you to do the same."
—Merle Feld, author of *A Spiritual Life*

The Sabbath Bee: Love Songs to Shabbat
by Wilhelmina Gottschalk

"Torah, say our sages, has seventy faces. As these prose poems reveal, so too does Shabbat. Here we meet Shabbat as familiar housemate, as the child whose presence transforms a family, as a spreading tree, as an annoying friend who insists on being celebrated, as a woman, as a man, as a bee, as the ocean."
—Rachel Barenblat, author, *The Velveteen Rabbi's Haggadah*

All the Holes Line Up: Poems and Translations
by Zackary Sholem Berger

"Spare and precise, Berger's poems gaze unflinchingly at—but also celebrate—human imperfection in its many forms. And what a delight that Berger also includes in this collection a handful of his resonant translations of some of the great Yiddish poets." —Yehoshua November, author of *God's Optimism* and *Two World Exist*

How to Bless the New Moon: The Priestess Paths Cycle and Other Poems for Queens
by Rachel Kann

"To read Rachel Kann's poems is to be confronted with the possibility that you, too, are prophet and beloved, touched by forces far beyond your mundane knowing. So, dear reader, enter into the 'perfumed forcefield' of these words—they are healing and transformative."
—Rabbi Jill Hammer, co-author of *The Hebrew Priestess*

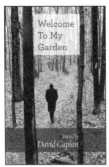

Into My Garden
by David Caplan

"The beauty of Caplan's book is that it is not polemical. It does not set out to win an argument or ask you whether you've put your tefillin on today. These gentle poems invite the reader into one person's profound, ambiguous religious experience."
— *The Jewish Review of Books*

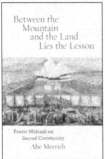

Between the Mountain and the Land is the Lesson: Poetic Midrash on Sacred Community
by Abe Mezrich

"Abe Mezrich cuts straight back to the roots of the Midrashic tradition, sermonizing as a poet, rather than idealogue. Best of all, Abe knows how to ask questions and avoid the obvious answers."
— Jake Marmer, author, *Jazz Talmud*

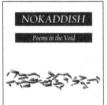

NOKADDISH: Poems in the Void
by Hanoch Guy Kaner

"A subversive, midrashic play with meanings—specifically Jewish meanings, and then the reversal and negation of these meanings."
— Robert G. Margolis

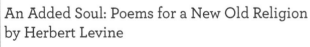

An Added Soul: Poems for a New Old Religion
by Herbert Levine

"These poems are remarkable, radiating a love of God that is full bodied, innocent, raw, pulsating, hot, drunk. I can hardly fathom their faith but am grateful for the vistas they open. I will sit with them, and invite you to do the same."
— Merle Feld, author of *A Spiritual Life*.

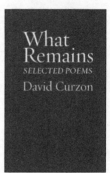

What Remains
by David Curzon

"Aphoristic, ekphrastic, and precise revelations animate WHAT REMAINS. In his stunning rewriting of Psalm 1 and other biblical passages, Curzon shows himself to be a fabricator, a collector, and an heir to the literature, arts, and wisdom traditions of the planet.
—Alicia Ostriker, author of *The Volcano and After*

The Shortest Skirt in Shul
by Sass Oron

"These poems exuberantly explore gender, Torah, the masks we wear, and the way our bodies (and the ways we wear them) at once threaten stable narratives, and offer the kind of liberation that saves our lives."
—Alicia Jo Rabins, author of *Divinity School*, composer of *Girls In Trouble*

Walking Triptychs
by Ilya Gutner

These are poems from when I walked about Shanghai and thought about the meaning of the Holocaust.

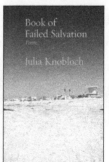

Book of Failed Salvation
by Julia Knobloch

"These beautiful poems express a tender longing for spiritual, physical, and emotional connection. They detail a life in movement—across distances, faith, love, and doubt."
—David Caplan, author, *Into My Garden*